NAME _____

SCHOOL _____

DATE _____

Book design by Alyssa Marie Publishing
Licensed graphics used with all appropriate commercial licenses. Add'l illustrations by Vecteezy.

CONTENTS

>>*Prompted title pages*

>>*Blank pages for notes, charts, lists, etc.*

❖ Blank Calendar - Good for any year
❖ Autographs
❖ Contacts
❖ Thoughts & Reflections

EACH QUARTER INCLUDES

❖ Best Friends
❖ Classes
❖ Clubs
❖ College Planning
❖ Events
❖ Goals
❖ Habit Tracker
❖ Hit Songs
❖ Memories
❖ Must See Movies
❖ Play Lists
❖ What's Trending
❖ You Tube Channels

Blank pages:
❖ Lined
❖ Graph

S	M	T	W	TH	F	S	S	M	T	W	TH	F	S	S	M	T	W	TH	F	S

JANUARY

FEBRUARY

MARCH

APRIL

MAY

JUNE

JULY

AUGUST

SEPTEMBER

OCTOBER

NOVEMBER

DECEMBER

IMPORTANT DATES

_____

| S | M | T | W | TH | F | S | S | M | T | W | TH | F | S | S | M | T | W | TH | F | S |

| JANUARY | FEBRUARY | MARCH |

| APRIL | MAY | JUNE |

| JULY | AUGUST | SEPTEMBER |

| OCTOBER | NOVEMBER | DECEMBER |

IMPORTANT DATES

Draw Something

QUARTER

1

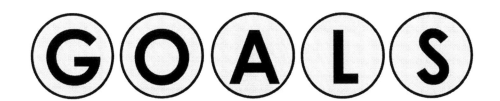

GOALS

✓

★ ⬜

★ ⬜

★ ⬜

● ⬜

● ⬜

● ⬜

● ⬜

● ⬜

● ⬜

● ⬜

● ⬜

● ⬜

● ⬜

#

Subject / Teacher ———————————————————

Notes & Memories ———————————————————

Subject / Teacher ———————————————————

Notes & Memories ———————————————————

Subject / Teacher ———————————————————

Notes & Memories ———————————————————

Classes

Subject / Teacher ....

Notes & Memories ....

Subject / Teacher ....

Notes & Memories ....

Subject / Teacher ....

Notes & Memories ....

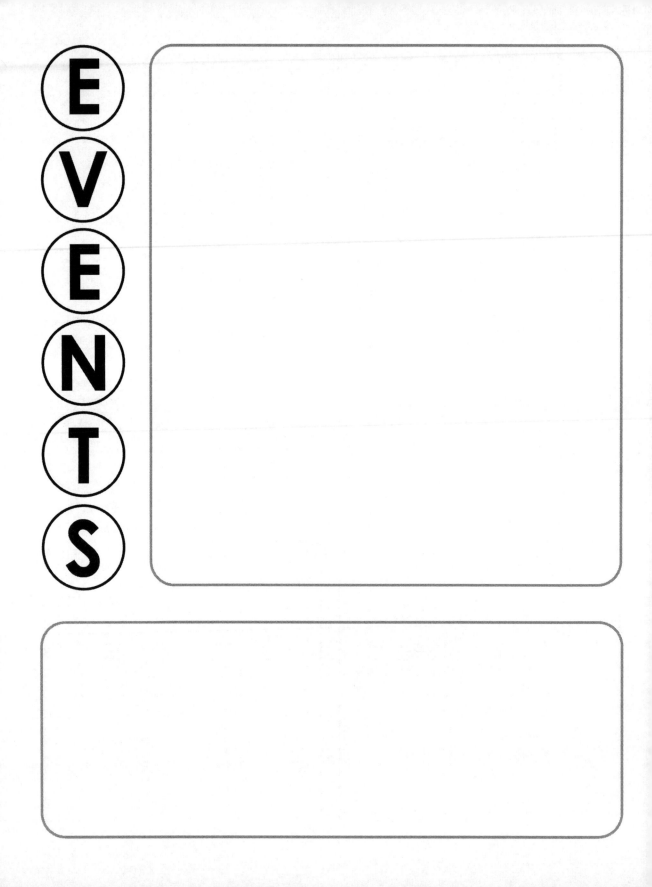

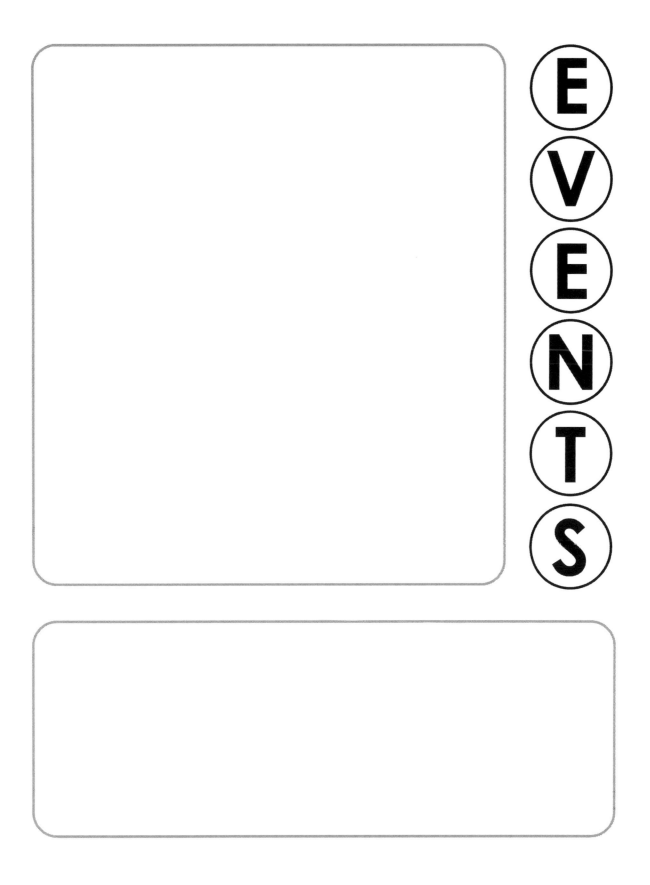

Trending

Hit Songs

PL▶YLISTS

Quotes to Remember

_____

_____

_____

_____

_____

says who: _____

_____

_____

_____

_____

says who: _____

_____

_____

_____

_____

says who: _____

Memorable Moments

Memorable Moments

Must See Movies

Best friends!

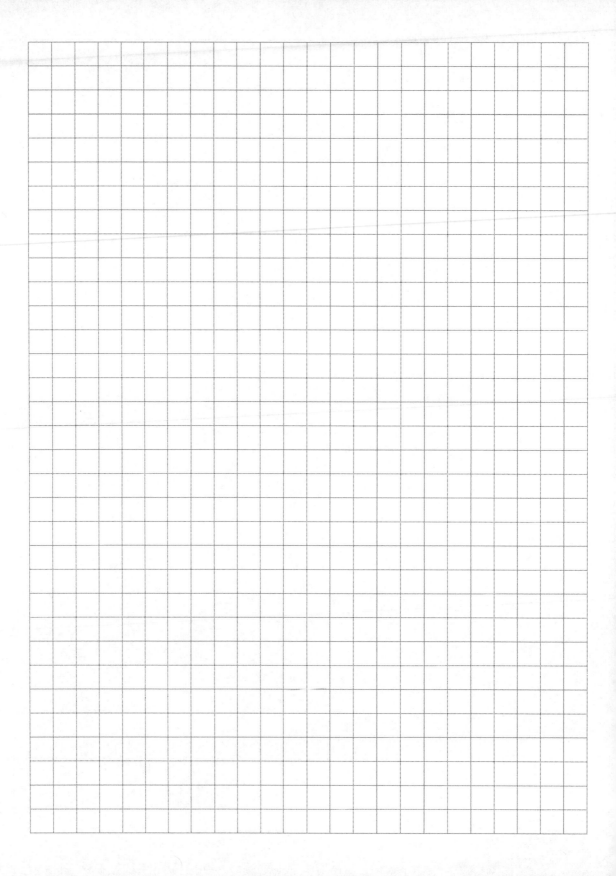

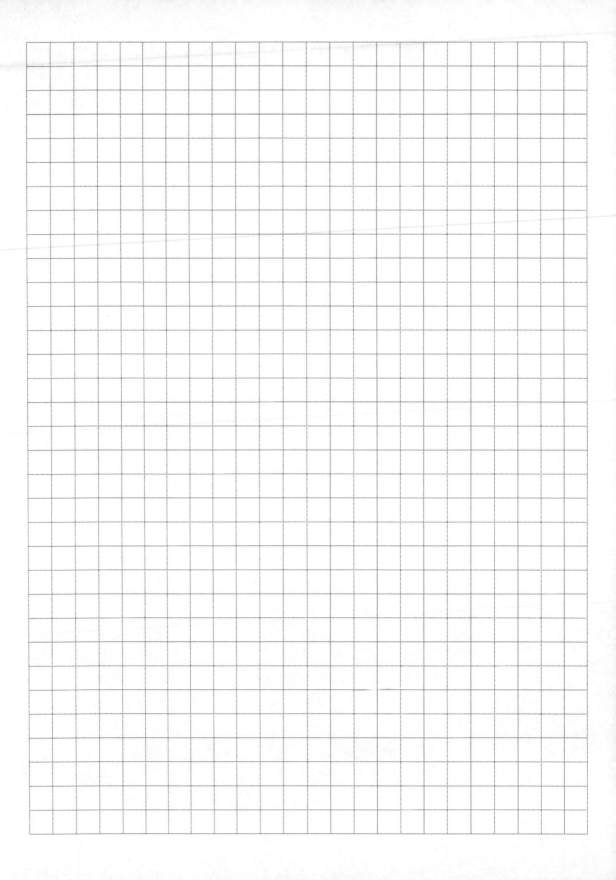

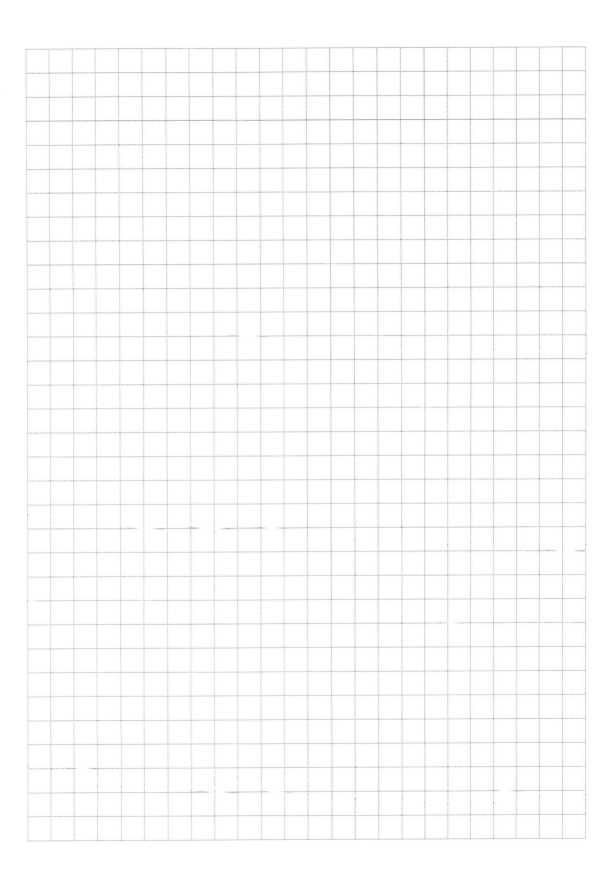

Habit Tracker

Habits - They make or break you

Habit Tracker

Habits - They make or break you

Draw Something

QUARTER

2

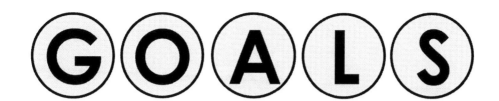

PRIORITIES

★ _____ ☐

★ _____ ☐

★ _____ ☐

✓

● _____ ☐

● _____ ☐

● _____ ☐

● _____ ☐

● _____ ☐

● _____ ☐

● _____ ☐

● _____ ☐

● _____ ☐

● _____ ☐

Classes

Subject / Teacher _____

Notes & Memories _____

Subject / Teacher _____

Notes & Memories _____

Subject / Teacher _____

Notes & Memories _____

Classes

Subject / Teacher ....

Notes & Memories ....

Subject / Teacher ....

Notes & Memories ....

Subject / Teacher ....

Notes & Memories ....

CLUBS

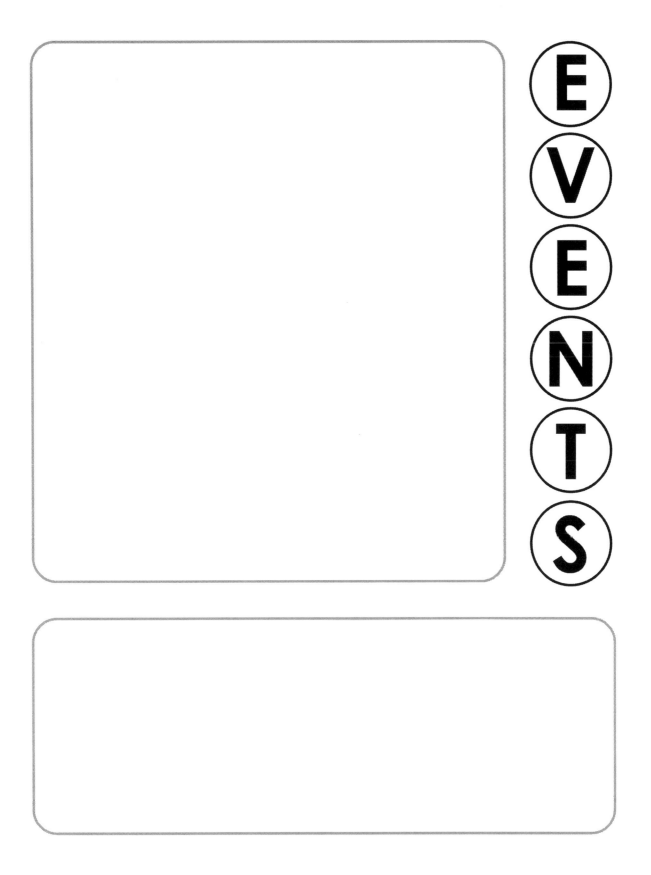

E
V
E
N
T
S

Trending

Hit Songs

PL▶YLISTS

Quotes to Remember

_____

_____

_____

_____

_____

_____

says who: _____

_____

_____

_____

_____

_____

says who: _____

_____

_____

_____

_____

_____

says who: _____

Memorable Moments

Memorable Moments

Must See Movies

Best friends!

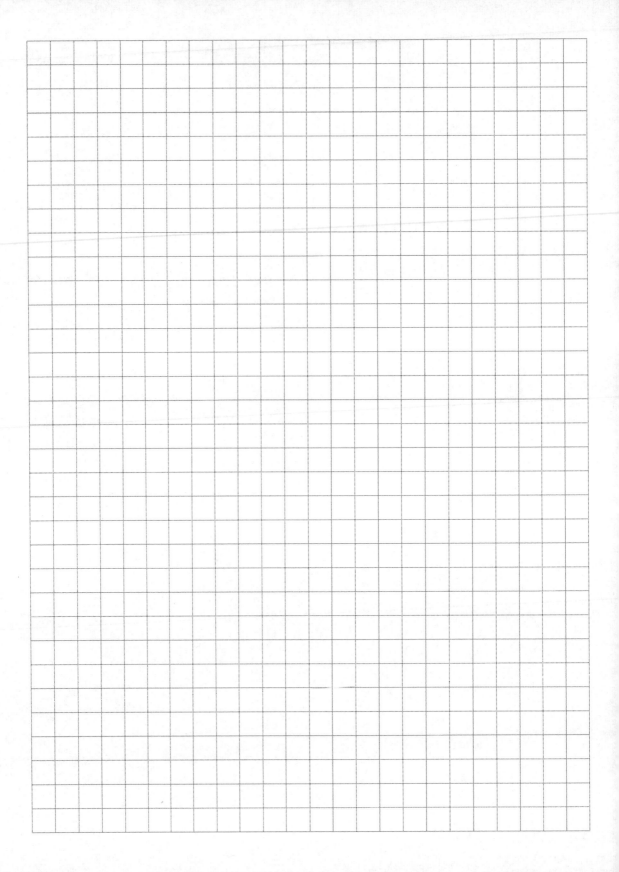

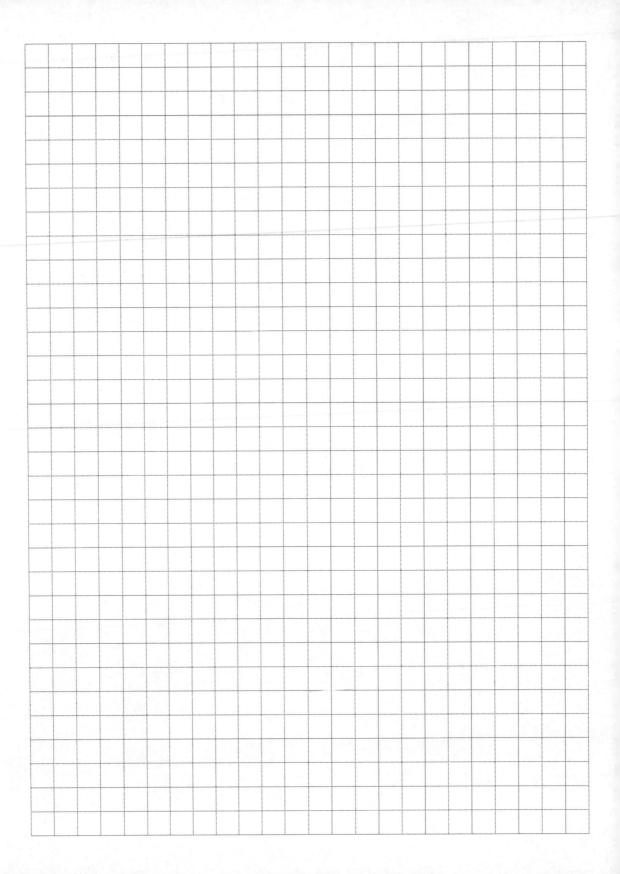

Habit Tracker

Habits - They make or break you

Habit Tracker

Habits - They make or break you

Draw Something

QUARTER

3

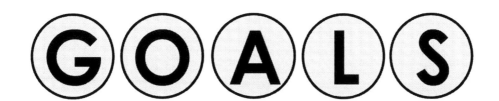

✓

★ _____ ☐

★ _____ ☐

★ _____ ☐

● _____ ☐

● _____ ☐

● _____ ☐

● _____ ☐

● _____ ☐

● _____ ☐

● _____ ☐

● _____ ☐

● _____ ☐

● _____ ☐

Classes

Subject / Teacher ————————————————————————————

Notes & Memories ————————————————————————————

Subject / Teacher ————————————————————————————

Notes & Memories ————————————————————————————

Subject / Teacher ————————————————————————————

Notes & Memories ————————————————————————————

Classes

Subject / Teacher ....

Notes & Memories ....

Subject / Teacher ....

Notes & Memories ....

Subject / Teacher ....

Notes & Memories ....

CLUBS

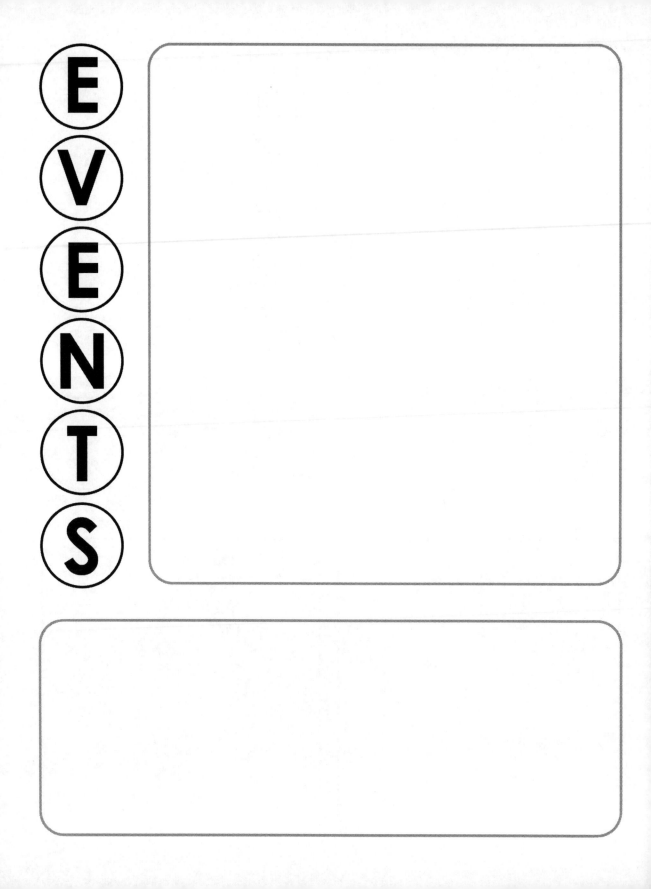

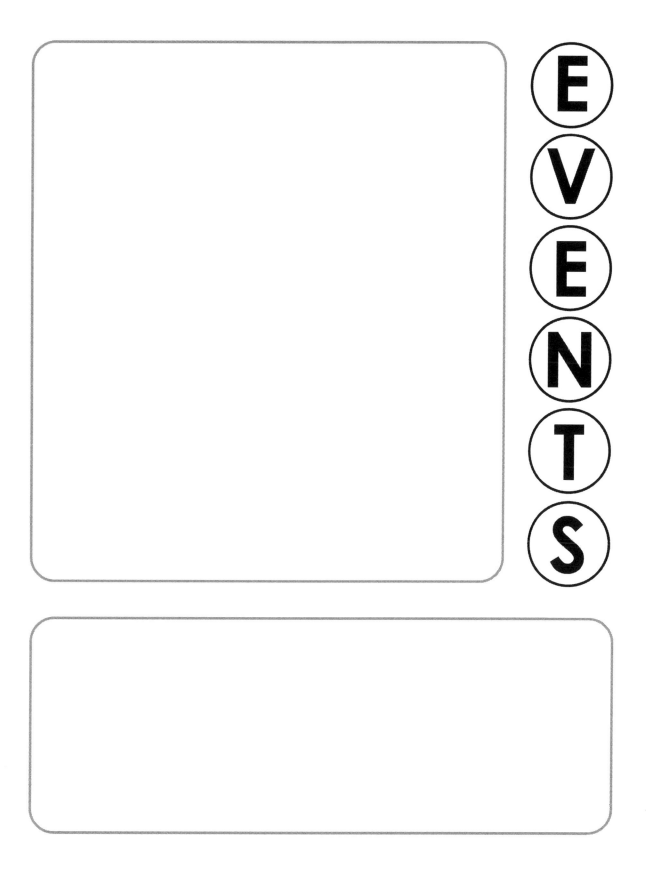

Trending

Hit Songs

PL▶YLISTS

|◄ ◄◄ _____ ►► ►| |◄ ◄◄ _____ ►► ►|

|◄ ◄◄ _____ ►► ►| |◄ ◄◄ _____ ►► ►|

Quotes to Remember

says who: _____

says who: _____

says who: _____

Memorable Moments

Memorable Moments

Must See Movies

Best friends!

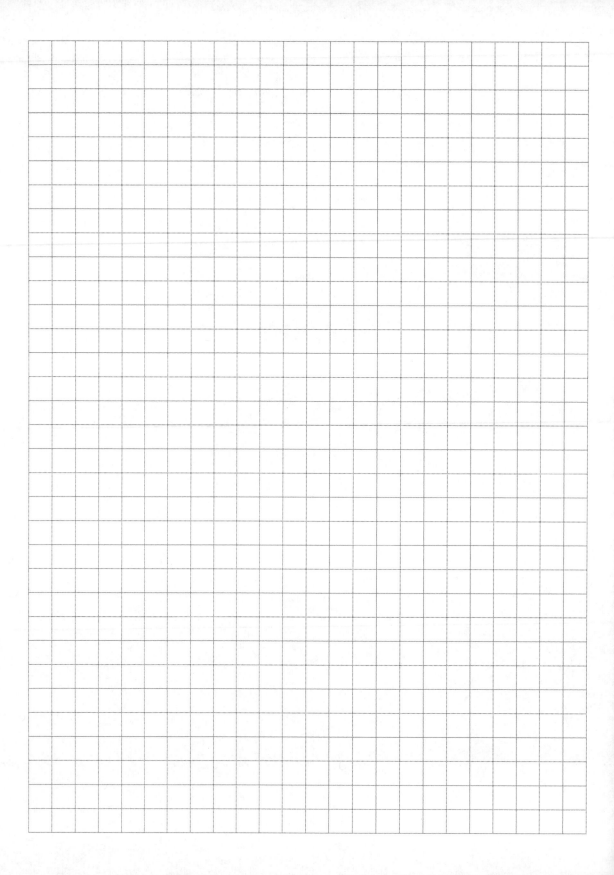

Habit Tracker

Habits - They make or break you

Habit Tracker

Habits - They make or break you

Draw Something

QUARTER

4

GOALS

✓

PRIORITIES

★ _____ ☐

★ _____ ☐

★ _____ ☐

● _____ ☐

● _____ ☐

● _____ ☐

● _____ ☐

● _____ ☐

● _____ ☐

● _____ ☐

● _____ ☐

● _____ ☐

● _____ ☐

Classes

Subject / Teacher ....

Notes & Memories ....

Subject / Teacher ....

Notes & Memories ....

Subject / Teacher ....

Notes & Memories ....

Classes

Subject / Teacher ....

Notes & Memories ....

Subject / Teacher ....

Notes & Memories ....

Subject / Teacher ....

Notes & Memories ....

CLUBS

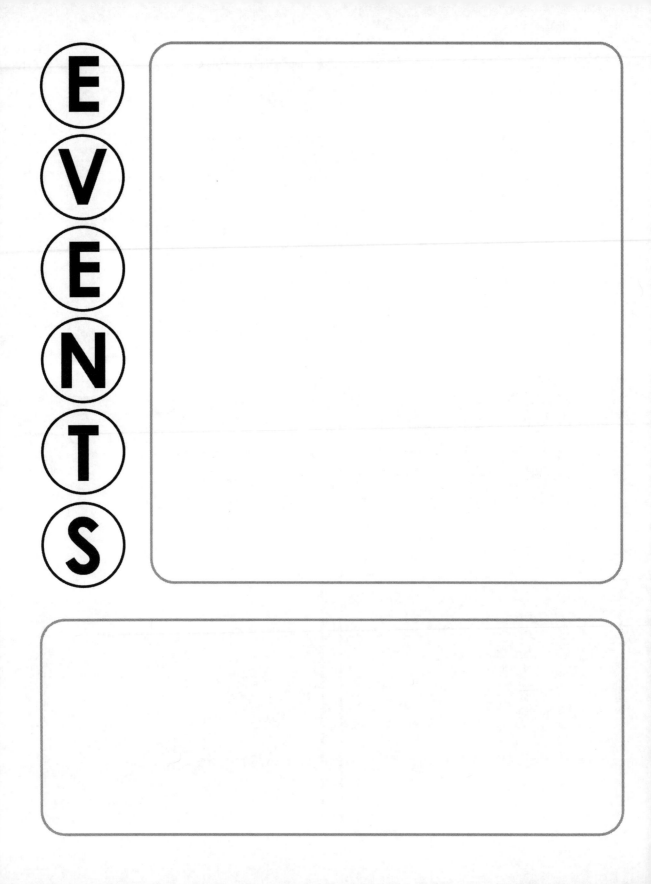

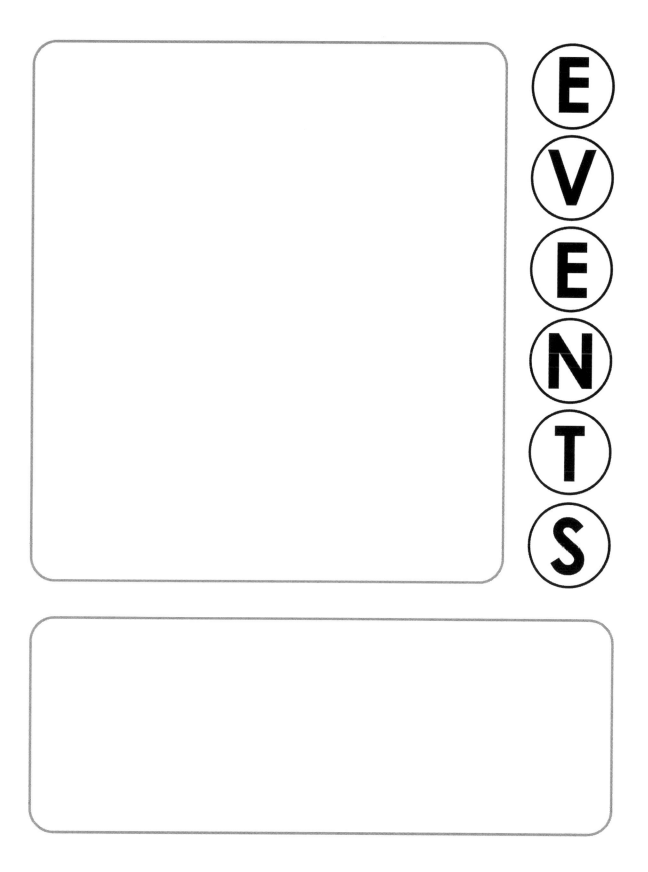

Trending

Hit Songs

PL▶YLISTS

⏮ ⏪ _____ ⏩ ⏭

⏮ ⏪ _____ ⏩ ⏭

⏮ ⏪ _____ ⏩ ⏭

⏮ ⏪ _____ ⏩ ⏭

▶ ▶| ◀))
_____

▶ ▶| ◀))
_____

Quotes to Remember

_____
_____
_____
_____
_____

says who: _____

_____
_____
_____
_____
_____

says who: _____

_____
_____
_____
_____
_____

says who: _____

Memorable
Moments

Memorable Moments

Must See Movies

Best friends!

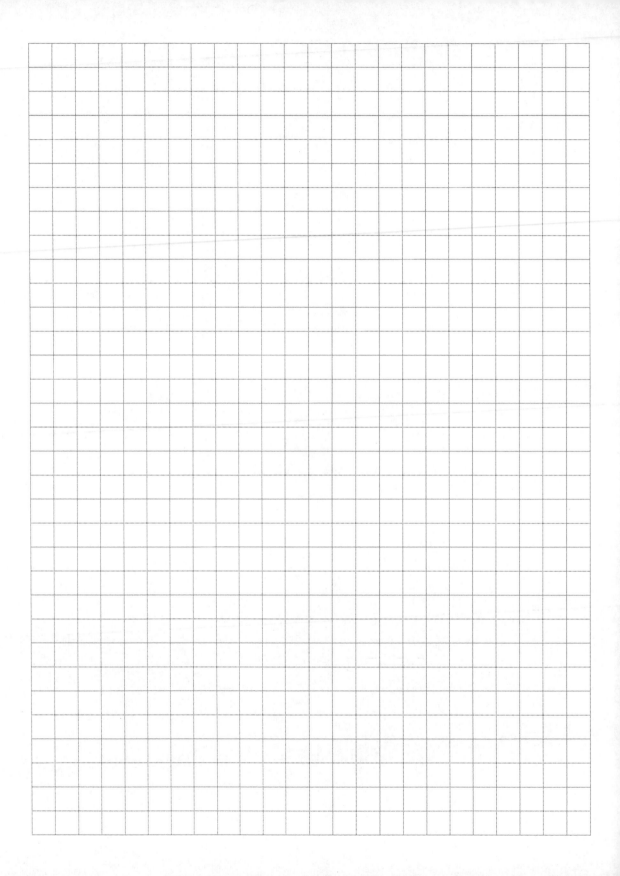

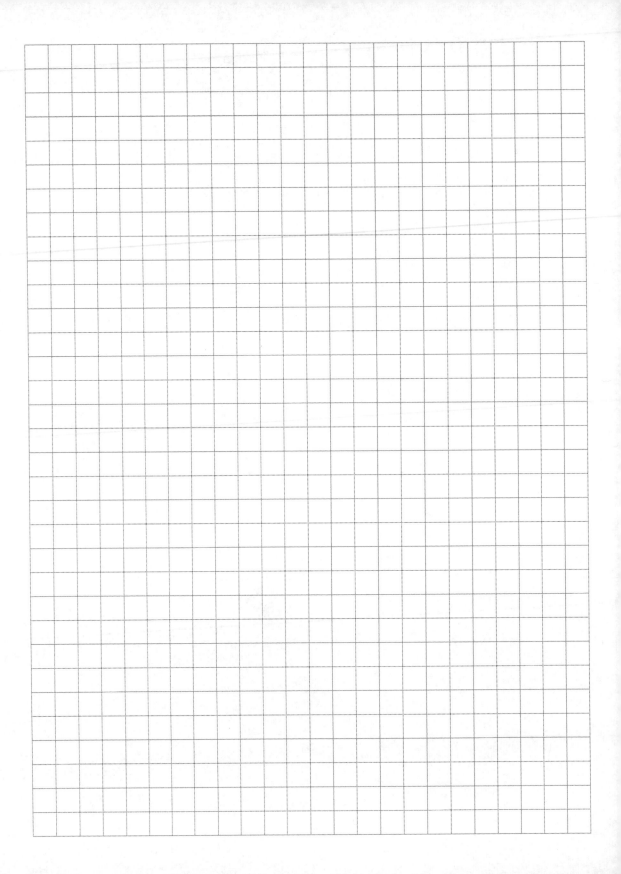

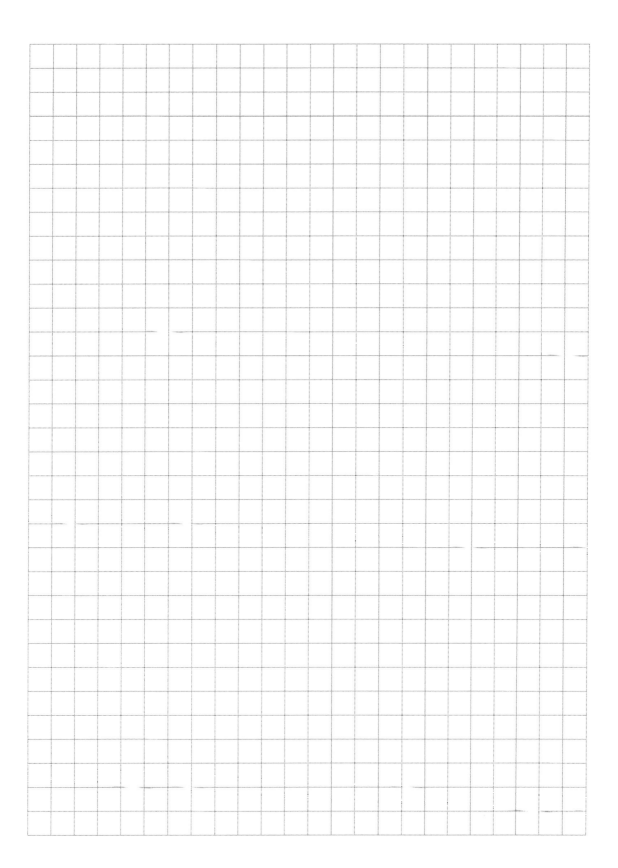

Habit Tracker

Habits - They make or break you

Habit Tracker

Habits - They make or break you

Draw Something

CONTACTS

CONTACTS

NAME | PHONE

SOCIAL MEDIA

NAME | PHONE

SOCIAL MEDIA

NAME | PHONE

SOCIAL MEDIA

NAME | PHONE

SOCIAL MEDIA

NAME | PHONE

SOCIAL MEDIA

CONTACTS

NAME | PHONE

SOCIAL MEDIA

NAME | PHONE

SOCIAL MEDIA

NAME | PHONE

SOCIAL MEDIA

NAME | PHONE

SOCIAL MEDIA

NAME | PHONE

SOCIAL MEDIA

CONTACTS

NAME

PHONE

SOCIAL MEDIA

NAME

PHONE

SOCIAL MEDIA

NAME

PHONE

SOCIAL MEDIA

NAME

PHONE

SOCIAL MEDIA

NAME

PHONE

SOCIAL MEDIA

CONTACTS

NAME

PHONE

SOCIAL MEDIA

NAME

PHONE

SOCIAL MEDIA

NAME

PHONE

SOCIAL MEDIA

NAME

PHONE

SOCIAL MEDIA

NAME

PHONE

SOCIAL MEDIA

CONTACTS

NAME   PHONE

SOCIAL MEDIA

NAME   PHONE

SOCIAL MEDIA

NAME   PHONE

SOCIAL MEDIA

NAME   PHONE

SOCIAL MEDIA

NAME   PHONE

SOCIAL MEDIA

CONTACTS

NAME

PHONE

SOCIAL MEDIA

NAME

PHONE

SOCIAL MEDIA

NAME

PHONE

SOCIAL MEDIA

NAME

PHONE

SOCIAL MEDIA

NAME

PHONE

SOCIAL MEDIA

Draw Something

Colleges

★ _____

★ _____

★ _____

• _____

• _____

• _____

• _____

• _____

• _____

• _____

• _____

• _____

• _____

Thoughts and Reflections

Summer Plans

Autographs

Autographs

Made in the USA
Middletown, DE
26 May 2020